FIRST LATIN

A LANGUAGE DISCOVERY PROGRAM

SECOND EDITION

LANGUAGE AND FAMILY

MARION POLSKY

STUDENT ACTIVITY BOOK I

Scott Foresman
Addison Wesley

Editorial Offices: Glenview, Illinois • Menlo Park, California
Sales Offices: Reading, Massachusetts • Atlanta, Georgia • Glenview, Illinois
Carrollton, Texas • Menlo Park, California

http://www.sf.aw.com

Consultants to the First Edition: John J. Langton, Professor Gilbert Lawall, Dr. Rudolph Masciantonio

Audio Cassette Performers: Dr. Marion Polsky, John J. Langton, Christine Ranck, Jay Berliner

Audio Cassette Producer: The Sun Group

First Latin, A Language Discovery Program, Student Activity Book I

Some of the art in the Cue Cards is based on art originally appearing in *First Latin: The Discovery of Language,* by Marion Polsky

ISBN: 0-673-21589-X

Contents

Welcome to Rome!

You may know the ancient Romans as people who ran around in togas and liked to watch gladiators fight lions. These are the Romans you see in the movies.

Who Were the Real Romans?

To begin with, they were people like us. They celebrated birthdays, wore wedding rings, went to the theater, worked for a living, took vacations, attended school, had parties, sent for the doctor, lived in houses or apartments, used cosmetics, bought presents, played sports, ate in fast-food restaurants, shopped, loved, argued, laughed, danced, and worshipped.

Roman children had dolls and toys, played ball games, and trained birds and mice as pets.

Romans celebrated many religious holidays, like the Saturnalia in honor of the god Saturn, Jupiter's father.

Romans liked to travel far and wide. They even visited the pyramids of Egypt and temples in ancient Greece.

Roman senators met in the Senate House to discuss government business and laws.

How Do We Know About the Ancient Romans Today?

The original Romans started out as farmers who built a village near the River Tiber in Italy almost three thousand years ago. The village grew, and Rome became a major city and trade center spread over seven hills. As time passed, Roman soldiers were sent to conquer nearby lands. Rome became a huge empire, with the city of Rome at its heart. The Roman Empire covered much of what we call Europe, northern Africa, and the Middle East today.

Although the Roman Empire no longer exists, we know a great deal about it from what the Romans left behind. The study of our past through old objects is called *archaeology.* Archaeologists, people who dig up what has been buried over time, have found Roman pots and pans, jewelry, coins, statues, paintings, tools, weapons, graves, even houses, theaters, race tracks, and temples. All of these things help us to understand the ancient Roman way of life.

Most important of all, the Romans had writing. And so they can tell us directly about themselves. From descriptions by ancient authors, written records found by archaeologists, and even graffiti on ancient buildings, we can recreate the history of Rome and the daily life of its men, women, and children.

Why Is It Important for Us to Learn About the Ancient Romans?

The Romans lived long ago, but they were great soldiers and builders. They left their mark on the history of the world. We owe much of our modern way of life to the Romans—our government and laws, our buildings, and the designs of our cities and roads. Most of all, the Romans gave us a language, Latin, which is basic to English. And Latin is the actual "parent" language of Spanish, French, and Italian, as you will see.

Although you may not realize it, you already know some Latin: *area, alibi, bonus, circus, color, data, error, gladiator, labor, medium, plus, rumor, senior, senator, series, stadium, vacuum,* and many other words look exactly the same in Latin and English. The motto of the United States is in Latin: **E pluribus unum** (one out of many). You can find it on the dollar bill.

The influence of Latin and the Romans is all around you. You can still see Roman ruins wherever the Romans built cities and, of course, in the modern city of Rome, Italy. But did you know that the Lincoln Memorial and the Capitol building in Washington, D.C. are based on Roman designs? And how about Yankee Stadium and other ball parks with ticket gates all around, like the famous Colosseum in Rome? Have you visited *Jupiter,* Florida, *Juno,* Alaska, *Cincinnati,* Ohio, or *Troy,* New York? Did you learn about the *Apollo* space missions? Have you seen a bride throw a bouquet? She is imitating Roman tradition.

As you study about the Romans and how they lived from day to day, you will be able to compare your own life-style with theirs. And along the way, you will speak the Latin language with your friends, read it, and write it, just as young Romans did! An adventure lies ahead for you, and lots of surprises. Get ready!

The Roman Experience

In this unit, you will:

learn to greet people in Latin, with your Latin name
identify places in the world in Latin
sing songs in Latin
read about Roman gods, heroes, and monsters
name the planets
solve Latin arithmetic problems
find out about city life in ancient Rome
act in Roman skits
read stories in Latin
discover the connection between Latin and English words

Rōmānī Antīquī

The Romans Tell Their Story

The Latin language, which you have been practicing, was originally spoken thousands of years ago by a people called the **Romans.** These ancient Romans built a great and powerful civilization.

Here are some famous figures from the Roman past, telling the story of Rome's beginnings and rise to power. Every Roman boy and girl knew by heart these tales of bravery, honor, and loyalty to Rome. Find the *name* of each speaker under his picture and copy it in the blank at the end of the speech.

Aeneas

"Over three thousand years ago, there was a great war between the **Greeks** and my people, the **Trojans,** who lived across the sea. I escaped with a small band of men, carrying my father on my back and clutching the hand of my small son. I traveled for 10 years, protected by my mother, the beautiful goddess **Venus.** I finally settled in **Italy,** in an area called Latium. There a people called the Latins were living. Their king, **Latinus,** gave me his daughter in marriage. The Trojans and the Latins soon became one nation, and I was the ruler. We all spoke **Latin,** the language of the Latin people."

_____

"My brother **Remus** and I were twins, sons of Rhea Silvia and the god of war, **Mars.** We came from the long bloodline of our great ancestor Aeneas. Our wicked uncle ordered us to be thrown into the Tiber River to drown, but we floated safely to a riverbank, where we were found and nursed by a she-wolf. Much later we returned to **Alba Longa,** our birthplace, killed our evil uncle, and put our grandfather **Numitor** back on the throne.

Romulus and Remus

"Remus and I left to build a *new city.* We argued because we both wanted to be king, but the gods sent me a special sign—twelve birds circling my head. **On April 21, 753 B.C.,** I built the walls of the city and named it **Roma,** after myself. When my brother mocked the walls, I killed him. No one would ever again scorn Rome, the great city of

_____."

Horatius

"Many years after Rome was built, the people drove out the last king, **Tarquin the Proud.** They wanted to be free, so in **509 B.C.** they set up a new form of government, a **republic,** with a constitution and elected officials. But a foreign king tried to put Tarquin back in power at Rome. While Rome was preparing for battle, I alone held off the king and all his forces at the head of a bridge. When the bridge was destroyed, I refused to surrender. Badly wounded, I leaped into the Tiber River and swam back to Rome in full armor."

_____.

"I swore to kill the same foreign king and sneaked into his camp. I was caught. To show how courageous we Romans are, I put my right hand on hot coals and burned it away. The king was impressed and decided to make peace with the Romans. I got the nickname **Scaevola,** 'Lefty.' "

Mucius Scaevola

_____.

Julius Caesar

"I was a great general, and probably the most famous Roman in history. I conquered many nations for Rome. I became so powerful that many citizens feared I would put an end to the Roman Republic. I was murdered on **March 15, 44 B.C.,** stabbed to death by my best friend, Brutus, and others in the Senate House."

_____.

"I, **Octavian,** was adopted by my great-uncle Julius Caesar and inherited his fortune after he was murdered. I had control of most of Rome and was able to bring about a long peace following many years of bloodshed between Romans. In **27 B.C.** I received

the supreme title _____,
which means 'the honored one,' and I am known in history by this name. The eighth month in the calendar is named for me. As the first emperor, I made Rome the greatest power in the Western world. The **Roman Empire** lasted 500 years."

Augustus

The Roman Empire

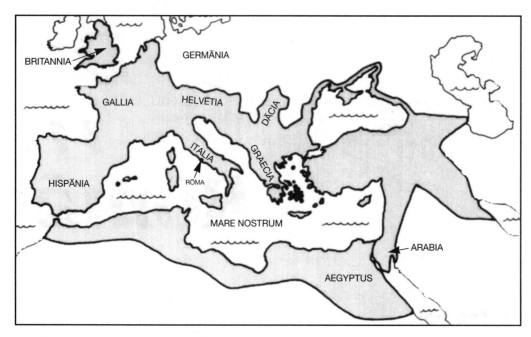

This is a map of the Roman Empire. The places have their Latin names.

1. Locate each place listed below and put its number on the map.
2. Next to each place on the list, put the modern English name.

You will see that many countries once were part of the Roman Empire. Today, Rome is still the largest city in Italy, but the Roman Empire no longer exists.

Ubi est . . . ?	Modern English Name
1. Italia	Italy
2. Hispānia	
3. Britannia	
4. Graecia	
5. Gallia	
6. Aegyptus	
7. Helvētia	Switzerland
8. Arabia	
9. Dācia	Romania
10. Mare Nostrum	Mediterranean Sea

Lingua Latīna

Latin is the mother of the **Romance** languages—Spanish, French, Italian, Portuguese, and Rumanian. These daughter languages developed in the parts of Europe that belonged to the Roman Empire. When the Romans conquered new lands, they brought their language, Latin, with them. Latin was the common language for all peoples living in the great Roman Empire.

Put the names of the Romance languages in the tree. Latin is the root.

You can see for yourself that the Romance languages are related to Latin:

Latin	Italian	French	Spanish	Portuguese	Rumanian
ūnus	uno	un	uno	um	un
duo	due	deux	dos	dois	doi
trēs	tre	trois	tres	trez	trei

How does **English** fit in?

English is not a Romance language. Its origins are in another mother language, **Germanic,** which is also the mother of modern German.

BUT—Latin vocabulary (words) entered the English language from its very beginning, and the process is still going on! *Computer, camera, video* all come from Latin. So, about three out of every five English words have Latin roots. Put ENGLISH in the section of the two trees that overlap:

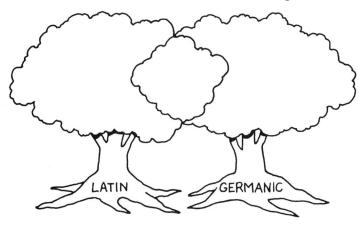

Rōma Est Magna!

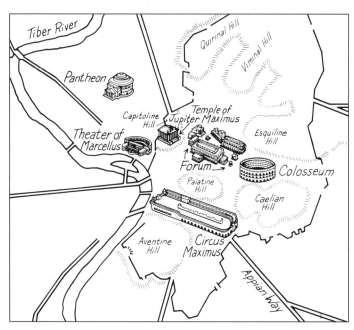

A Tour of the City

If you lived in the city of Rome about 110 A.D., you might meet Lucius, who is eleven years old. His cousin Cornelia is visiting from Abellinum, a small town in southern Italy. The two are discussing the sights and planning a tour. This is Cornelia's first trip to the big city.

As you read, think about buildings and places in your own home town which may be like the ones described here.

CORNELIA: "I can't believe I'm finally here! I want to see everything—the Colosseum, the Circus Maximus, the Temple of Jupiter, the Palace of Augustus, the Theater of Marcellus, and the Baths of our wonderful Emperor Trajan. And, of course, the Forum for shopping. How about a picnic on the banks of the Tiber River, too?"

LUCIUS: "Hold on, hold on! Nobody can visit all those places in one day. **Rōma est magna!** You saw that for yourself when you arrived. By the way, how did you get here?"

CORNELIA: "I came in a carriage with some other travelers from the South. We took the Appian Way, of course. I saw tombs all along the roadside; many had lifelike statues of the dead. They scared me a little. I admit I was impressed by the huge aqueduct leading into the city. I guess it's true that we Romans are great engineers."

LUCIUS: "I can see you are excited. I'm proud of my city. It's the center of the whole Empire. As the saying goes, **'Omnēs viae Rōmam dūcunt'**— 'All roads lead to Rome!' I'll tell you about some of the sights you mentioned, and then you can decide what to see first, okay?"

Here are the places that Lucius described:

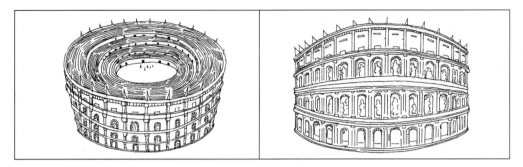

The most famous sight in Rome, the **Colosseum** was a huge, round building in the center of the city. Spectators watched gladiatorial contests and fights between all kinds of wild animals—lions, hippos, elephants, ostriches, and giraffes, to name a few. There were even combats between animals and men. Children would not generally be taken to these, but they might see naval battles or ship races in which the whole floor of the amphitheater was flooded with water from underground pipes. The Colosseum could hold 50,000 people.

The very first Roman race course, the **Circus Maximus,** was the biggest of the three in the city, a gigantic 1,800 feet long and 600 feet wide. Here, Lucius and his family would watch chariot races and root for their favorite team—the Reds, Greens, Blues, or Whites. It could seat 250,000 people! **Circus** in Latin means "ring."

Plays were performed at the **Theater of Marcellus** for 12,000 spectators during holidays, when schools and businesses were closed. Actors wore masks that indicated to the audience who their characters were. Audiences were so noisy that pantomimes became popular. These had dancing, singing, and a live orchestra, and were acted out without words.

The busiest place in all of Rome, the **Forum** was the heart of Roman business life, government, and religious activity. Here visitors would see the Black Stone, which marked the spot where Romulus was buried, the Curia, where Lucius' father and other senators met, and the enormous Temple of Saturn, father of Jupiter, the king of the gods. There were the Basilica Julia or law court, built by Julius Caesar, the beautiful temple of Vesta, and many shops lining the main street, like a mall.

Near the Forum was the Palatine Hill, where the Palace of Augustus and houses of other wealthy people were located. Looking down upon the Forum from the Capitoline Hill was the magnificent temple of Jupiter Maximus.

The Forum was crowded and noisy, with street vendors selling snacks, acrobats and other entertainers trying to earn a few coins, and rich people mixing with poor to get their daily business done. Tourists like Cornelia would see people from all over the Empire, differing in the color of their eyes, hair, and skin and wearing a variety of clothing styles. She would hear many different languages, too, for the Roman Empire was large, and Romans made up a world community.

∿∿

Time Traveler: Lucius Visits Your Town

Imagine that Lucius and Cornelia have arrived in your town by a magic time machine. What would you show them? How would you compare the sights to those in ancient Rome? What new types of buildings and public entertainment would surprise them? Write down your guided tour, starting with the most important places.

∿∿

Naming in Ancient Rome

Roman men and boys had three names:

1. the **praenōmen,** similar to our first or given name.
2. the **nōmen,** similar to our last name. This was the clan name. All free-born Romans belonged to a clan, or large family group.
3. the **cognōmen,** which indicated a particular family within the larger clan. We do not have this category of name in our system.

Here is an example:

Marcus	*Tullius*	*Cicero*
praenōmen	nōmen	cognōmen

Daughter: Tullia
Son: Marcus Tullius Cicero

You will notice that the daughter simply has the father's **nōmen,** with a feminine ending *-a.* What was Cornelia's father's **nōmen?**

_____

If a family had more than one daughter, the girls were named by birth order: **Tullia Prīma** (first-born), **Tullia Secunda** (second-born), and so on. When the daughters got married, they sometimes added their husband's **nōmen** as their second name.

Sons often took their father's **praenōmen,** as in the example. More often, though, a boy's **praenōmen** stood for his birth order: **Prīmus, Secundus,** and so on. In fact, there were very few different first names in ancient Rome, compared to names today.

Here are some *actual* Roman names, either first names or clan names. Put the modern English version next to the Latin name:

Antōnius _____   Aemilia _____

Claudia _____   Marcus _____

Iūlius _____   Iūlia _____

Many other English names come from real Latin *words.* Here are some: Alma, Amanda, Amy, Beatrice, Belle, Felix, Florence, Grace, Leo, Margaret, Max, Paul, Peter, Rose, Stella, Sylvia, Vera, Victor, Victoria, Vincent. You can find out the *meaning* of these names and the Latin words they come from by looking in an English dictionary.

What does *your* real first name mean? _____

What does your **praenōmen** in the class mean? _____

In Urbe

Duae Puellae

It is 6:00 A.M. sunrise. Lucius' sister, Claudia, who is 13, awakens her cousin.

CLAUDIA: "How did you sleep, Cornelia?"

CORNELIA: "To tell you the truth, not too well. There was a lot of noise outside—people shouting and singing until all hours, and wagon wheels clanking on the cobblestones all night."

CLAUDIA: "Oh, the people must have been guests coming home from our neighbor Trimalchio's big party. They probably drank too much wine! It's too bad we live near a major road. The work wagons use it to bring food and supplies to the city, but they're allowed to enter Rome only at night. I guess I'm used to the sound. Wake up, now! Let's go to the Forum."

Claudia, Cornelia, and Lucius leave the house early, grabbing breakfast on the way—a sweet flat pancake at the baker's. In a building near the Forum, Cornelia hears some boys screaming and a man yelling at them.

LUCIUS: "Uh-oh! Orbilius is in a bad mood, and I'm late."

CLAUDIA: "Better hurry up, **Lūcī.** Orbilius is the schoolteacher, Cornelia. He is very strict and sometimes hits his students. Good luck, **Lūcī! Valē!**"

Lucius goes into the schoolroom. The two girls enter the Forum.

CORNELIA: "I can't believe there are so many people in one place. Look at the dancers, Claudia! Why are they here? And what's that animal?"

CLAUDIA: "That's a baboon, a very rare pet! It belongs to the rich banker Fulvius. See him lying in that fancy litter, being carried by slaves all dressed up in silk and jewels? He likes to show off. Let's go see the acrobat. He's my favorite street entertainer."

CORNELIA: "Wait up, Claudia! I want to have my fortune told."

CLAUDIA: "No, Cornelia, be careful. Those fortune-tellers will try to cheat you. Look! There's a funeral procession right on the Via Sacra. The women are wailing and the trumpets are blasting. I can hardly hear. Let's hurry past them and get to the Rostra; maybe Aulus is giving a speech on the latest political scandal. Speakers at this spot like to yell out to the senators and other officials as they enter the Curia."

CORNELIA: "I noticed some soldiers across the way. People are cheering."

CLAUDIA: "Yes, they're back from a foreign war fought for our Emperor Trajan. They'll have a big victory parade tomorrow. Would you like to see the shops?"

As the two girls walk along the shopping arcade, they see people of different nationalities and races selling wonderful goods from all over the world.

CORNELIA: "Look at that fine blue silk. It would make a great **stola** for the banquet your father is giving in my honor."

CLAUDIA: "We'll see. I want to go to the goldsmith's shop for new earrings."

Tired from shopping, the cousins decide to get a snack at the nearest food stand. They settle on smoked fish, cheese, bread, and some wine.

CORNELIA: "Claudia, I'm exhausted. The crowds are enormous. I've never seen so many pushy people. The screaming is giving me a headache. Let's take our food and find a nice shady spot for a picnic. It's noon, and the sun is hot."

CLAUDIA: "Relax, Cornelia. Everybody's on edge by this hour. Soon all the shops and government houses will close down. Let's walk to the Baths. We'll eat our lunch on the way."

CORNELIA: "Perhaps we should walk north. Somebody told me the Subura district is nice."

CLAUDIA: "Oh, Cornelia, you have a lot to learn. The Subura is a very rough neighborhood, too dangerous to walk around in. And it's out of our way."

On the way to the Baths, the girls find themselves on a narrow street.

CLAUDIA: "Watch out, Cornelia! Here comes a carriage. Press yourself against this building, so it can pass."

CORNELIA: "I'm not used to such cramped spaces in my village. It's nice and quiet there and—Oh, no! Oh, no! Someone just spilled filthy cooking water on me from that apartment window. See it?"

CLAUDIA: "Oh, I'm sorry. I forgot to warn you about that. We should walk in the middle of the street. People sometimes do throw their garbage out the window. You have to watch where you step!"

At the Baths, the two meet Claudia's friend, Livia. They have a wonderful time, washing, swimming, and gossiping.

CLAUDIA: "We have to go home now. It's a long walk. Mother is expecting us for dinner. Besides, I don't have a torch to light our way once it gets dark."

CORNELIA: "Okay, Claudia. I hate to leave, though. These are the most beautiful baths I've ever seen; the marble and statues are really lovely."

CLAUDIA: "Yes, they are. Now I can't wait to take you to the theater and the races and other sights. How do you like Rome so far?"

CORNELIA: "Well, Claudia, it's exciting—full of things to do and interesting people and places. Everything's so big compared to where I live. Rome is a nice place to visit, but—I wouldn't want to live here."

CLAUDIA: "Little cousin, **dē gustibus nōn est disputandum.** But I bet you'll change your mind."

FINIS

∽∿∿∿∿∿∿∿∿∿∿∿∿∿∿∿∿∿∿∿∿∿∿∿∿∿∿∿∿∿∿∿∿∿

Then and Now: City Living

Find ten features of everyday life in ancient Rome that you might also find in a typical modern American city. Here's one to get you started: *crowds.*

∽∿∿∿∿∿∿∿∿∿∿∿∿∿∿∿∿∿∿∿∿∿∿∿∿∿∿∿∿∿∿∿∿∿

Fābella: Trēs Puellae

Persōnae: Claudia, Cornēlia, Līvia

CLAUDIA: Salvē, Līvia! (1)

LĪVIA: Salvē, Claudia! *(turning to Cornelia)* Salvē! Quid est praenōmen tibi? Quis es? (2)

CORNĒLIA: Salvē! Praenōmen mihi est Cornēlia. Consōbrīna Claudiae sum. (3)
  Quid est praenōmen tibi? (4)

LĪVIA: Praenōmen mihi est Līvia. Puella Rōmāna sum. Amīca Claudiae sum. (5)

Livia and Cornelia shake hands. The three girls walk to the Baths.

Vocabulary Help:

 (3) **consōbrīna Claudiae** Claudia's cousin
 (5) **amīca Claudiae** Claudia's friend

For boys' version, substitute these names: Claudius, Līvius, Cornēlius. Also change:
line 1—Salvē, Līvī!
line 2—Salvē, Claudī!
line 3—consōbrīnus Claudī
line 5—Puer Rōmānus sum. Amīcus Claudī sum.

Word Play: Camera Nostra

In the picture above, find the Latin word for each of the following and write it in the blank:

1. teacher   _____magistra_____

2. student (boy)   _____

3. desk/table   _____

4. chair   _____

5. door   _____

6. window   _____

7. wall   _____

8. room   _____

9. flag   _____

10. clock   _____

11. picture   _____

12. board   _____

13. chalk   _____

14. eraser   _____

15. pen   _____

16. pencil   _____

17. paper   _____

18. ruler   _____

Mini-Review I

Praenōmen mihi est _____.

True or False?

Mark each statement below TRUE or FALSE.

1. _____ The Roman Forum was the center for business and government.

2. _____ Lucius watched acrobats and clowns in the Circus Maximus.

3. _____ In the Forum, Cornelia saw Fulvius, a banker, and his pet baboon.

4. _____ Ancient Rome was built on nine hills.

5. _____ The Subura was a wealthy district of the city.

6. _____ Romans went to the baths to relax and meet friends after work.

7. _____ Roman actors wore masks on stage.

8. _____ A Roman man's *first* name was his **nōmen.**

9. _____ The Latin word for chair is **mēnsa.**

10. _____ You write with a **stilus** or **penna.**

Word Search: Roman Heroes

Find and circle the Latin names of the people and gods described below. Words may go across, down, or on the diagonal, but are never backward.

1. brother of Romulus
2. king of the Latins
3. founder of Rome
4. mother of Aeneas
5. "Lefty"
6. father of Romulus
7. first emperor of Rome
8. Julius _____, a great general
9. hero at a bridge
10. Trojan who came to Italy

```
H  O  R  A  T  I  U  S
A  C  M  A  R  S  I  A
U  A  P  R  O  R  L  E
G  E  N  L  S  O  A  N
U  S  T  R  V  M  T  E
S  A  D  E  E  U  I  A
T  R  A  M  N  L  N  S
U  C  U  U  U  U  U  U
S  S  S  S  S  S  S  S
```

Ubi Est . . . ?

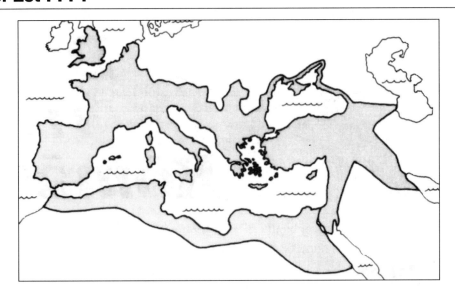

1. Find the modern English name for each place listed below and put it in the first column.

England   Spain   Egypt   Italy   Romania   France   Germany   Greece

Latin Name	English Name	Language
Italia	_____	_____
Britannia	_____	_____
Gallia	_____	_____
Hispānia	_____	_____
Aegyptus	_____	_____
Dācia	_____	_____
Graecia	_____	_____
Germānia	_____	_____

2. In the second column above, place the name of the language now spoken in each country.

German   French   Spanish   Italian   Rumanian   Arabic   Greek   English

3. Put circles around the names of the four **Romance languages** in the column. Then complete this sentence: The mother of these languages is

_____, which was the common language for all peoples

living in the great _____ Empire.

Ūnus, Duo, Trēs Rōmānī

Numerī Rōmānī

In many civilizations, the fingers of the human hand are used for counting from 1 to 10. The Romans created their written numerals from this method of counting:

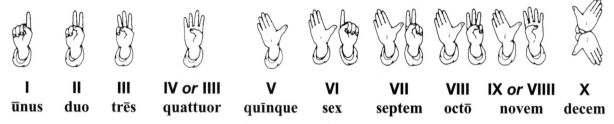

I	II	III	IV *or* IIII	V	VI	VII	VIII	IX *or* VIIII	X
ūnus	**duo**	**trēs**	**quattuor**	**quīnque**	**sex**	**septem**	**octō**	**novem**	**decem**

Count the objects in each row. Then put the Roman numeral in the first blank and the Latin word for the number in the second blank:

1. ☐☐☐☐☐ ____V____ ____quīnque____

2. ●●●△△△△ _____ _____

3. ◆ _____ _____

4. ○○▼▼▼☐ _____ _____

5. ◇◇◇◇ _____ _____

6. ▲▼▲▼▲▼▲▼ _____ _____

7. ◆◆◆△△△△ _____ _____

8. ■■ _____ _____

9. △▽△▽△▽△▽ _____ _____

10. ●●● _____ _____

Word Play

By now you have seen that many English words can come from just one Latin word. Each Latin word has a root-form, and it is this form that is used to make English words. For example, **ūnus** (one) has the root-form **ūni-**.

In this book, each time a Latin word is presented for word study, the root-form of it will also be given to you. This form always ends in a hyphen to show you that it is not a word by itself, but it goes into making an English word.

Here are the root-forms for the numbers 1 to 4 in Latin:

(ūnus) ūni-   (duo) du-   (trēs) tri-   (quattuor) quadr-

You are now ready to build new words:

1. If a *quadrilateral* figure is a figure with *four* sides (from Latin **later-**, "side"),

    how many sides does a *trilateral* have? _____.

2. If a *triangle* has *three* angles, what is the word for a figure with *four*

    angles? _____.

3. If a *tricycle* is a vehicle with *three* wheels, what is the word for a vehicle

    with *one* wheel? _____.
    As you know, a vehicle with two wheels is a *bicycle.* This word has a different Latin root that also means "two": **bi-** (Latin **bis,** "twice") + **cycle. Bi-** is used more often than **du-** to make English words.

4. If something that has two shapes is *biform,* what is the word for something

    that has *one* shape? _____.

    Three shapes? _____.

5. **Pod-** and **ped-** are roots that mean "foot." How many feet does a *biped*

    have? _____ A *unipod?* _____ A *tripod?* _____

    A *quadruped?* _____.

6. The ending **-ple** (sometimes **-uple**) means "times." If you make something

    four times bigger, you *quadruple* it. If you make it *three* times bigger, you

    _____ it. But twice as big is *double,* not **biple!*

Word Game

I've Got Your Number

For each number set, choose the word from the list at the top that best completes each sentence.

Ūnus, Ūni-

UNILATERAL   UNITY   UNICORN   UNIFORM

1. A treaty that is one-sided is called a _____ agreement.

2. A mythological creature that has a horn on its head is a

   _____.

3. Mary baked all the cookies the same size to make them

   _____.

4. When Jim and Al agreed, they expressed a _____ of opinion.

Trēs, Tri-

TRIANGLE   TRIPLICATE   TRICOLOR   TRICEPS

1. A geometrical figure with three angles is a _____.

2. The three-headed muscle in the back of the upper arm is the

   _____.

3. The French flag, which is blue, white, and red, is called the

   _____.

4. Important reports are often made up in _____.

Quattuor, Quadr-

QUADRANGLE   QUADRUPED   QUADRUPLET   QUADRILATERAL

1. A human being is a biped, but a horse or a cow is a _____.

2. A figure with four sides is a _____.

3. A figure having four angles is called a _____.

4. A baby who is one of four born at the same time is a _____.

Unicorns and Other Mythological Creatures

Roman children did not have picture books at home, but they heard the stories of heroes like Aeneas and Horatius from their parents. Myths were also popular—stories about gods, goddesses, and the human beings they met. Some myths helped to explain how nature works: for example, why there are seasons, where the sun goes when it sets, what thunder is. Myths also described human behavior—why people do the things they do. The heroes and heroines of ancient Greek and Roman mythology had remarkable adventures filled with strange monsters and magic. They were as familiar to Lucius, Cornelia, and Claudia as characters like Peter Pan, Cinderella, and Superman are to you.

In most of these stories, strange mythological creatures appeared. Some were everyday animals with strange forms, like unicorns or Pegasus, the winged horse. Others were combinations of humans and animals. Label the combinations under the pictures of the following creatures. Choose from the list provided. (Some choices are used more than once.)

bird	bull	dragon	goat	horse	lion	man	woman

Centaur

Harpy

_____ _____

Minotaur

Chimera

_____ _____

_____ _____

_____

Here are some other famous mythological creatures. Find their unusual feature in the following list: **ūnus oculus, tria capita, sex capita.** Write it underneath the name.

| Cerberus | Scylla | Cyclops |

Questions to Think About:

1. Why do imaginary creatures and monsters appear in myths?
2. Do heroes today fight strange creatures or monsters? Name some.
3. Look up the stories of the heroes who conquered or killed the creatures pictured on these pages: Aeneas, Bellerophon, Hercules, Theseus, Ulysses.

Using the Dictionary

Sometimes you may *think* that a particular English word comes from a Latin root you recognize. But how do you know for sure? To find out, you have to look in a good dictionary that contains information on the history of the English word. This information is enclosed in brackets like these: [   ]

Here's an example:

unicorn—a mythical creature usually represented as a horse with a single horn. [Middle English, from Old French, from Latin **ūnicornis: ūni-** "one" + **cornū** "horn"]

Do you seen the **ūni-** in the bracketed section?

Sometimes the names of the languages will be abbreviated. Look for **Latin, L, LL,** or **Lat** to prove that the English word comes from Latin.

Now try the dictionary yourself. Look up these English words to find the Latin roots:

binoculars _____

triceps _____

uniform _____

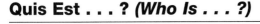

Rōmānus, Rōmāna

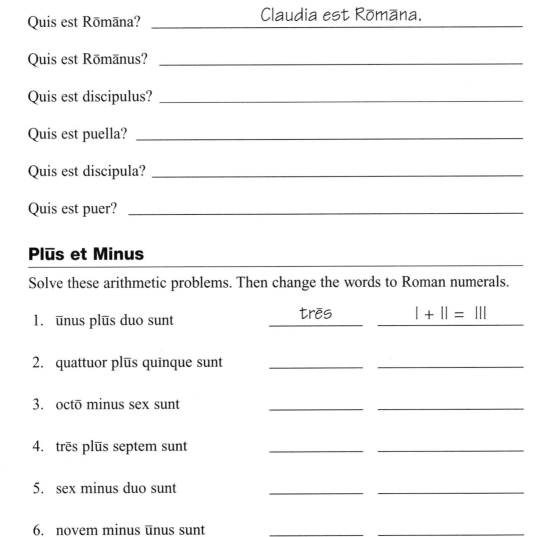

Quis Est . . . ? (Who Is . . . ?)

Lūcius et Claudia sunt duo Rōmānī.

Quis est Lūcius? Quis est Claudia?

Write out sentences as answers to the following questions
in the space provided. Start your sentence with either **Lūcius** or **Claudia:**

Quis est Rōmāna? _____ Claudia est Rōmāna. _____

Quis est Rōmānus? _____

Quis est discipulus? _____

Quis est puella? _____

Quis est discipula? _____

Quis est puer? _____

Plūs et Minus

Solve these arithmetic problems. Then change the words to Roman numerals.

1. ūnus plūs duo sunt _____ trēs _____   _____ I + II = III _____

2. quattuor plūs quīnque sunt _____   _____

3. octō minus sex sunt _____   _____

4. trēs plūs septem sunt _____   _____

5. sex minus duo sunt _____   _____

6. novem minus ūnus sunt _____   _____

7. duo multiplicātum per trēs sunt _____   _____

8. decem dīvīsum per duo sunt _____   _____

Roman Calendar

Iānuārius est prīmus mēnsis.

Februārius est secundus mēnsis.

Martius est tertius mēnsis.

Aprīlis est quārtus mēnsis.

Māius est quintus mēnsis.

Iūnius est sextus mēnsis.

Iūlius est septimus mēnsis.

Augustus est octāvus mēnsis.

September est nōnus mēnsis.

Octōber est decimus mēnsis.

November est ūndecimus mēnsis.

December est duodecimus mēnsis.

Janus was the god of doorways and of beginnings. What month is his?

As you can see, the names of our months come from the Roman calendar.

The Roman year used to begin with the month of **Martius** (March). For this reason, the *seventh* month was September, from **septem.** After January and February were added to the beginning of the year, September became the ninth month of the year instead of the seventh.

November is the eleventh month. How can you tell that **ūndecimus** means "eleventh"? Hint: Divide the word into its two parts and add them together. *December* is the twelfth month. Explain how **duodecimus** means "twelfth."

The numbers that you see in front of the word **mēnsis** (month) are called *ordinal* numbers because they show the *order* of the months from first to twelfth. Give in Latin:

fourth month _____ quārtus mēnsis _____

second month _____

eighth month _____

first month _____

Remember the story of the founding of Rome? Answer in Latin:

Quis est **prīmus** Rōmānus? _____

Word Play

The ordinal numbers give us more root-forms for number words in English:

prīm-   **second-**   **quārt-**   **quīnt-**   **sext-**   **octāv-**   **decim-**
I   II   IV   V   VI   VIII   X

Here is a list of the most important Latin root-forms for 1 to 10. Next to each root is an example of an English word based on it:

I.	**ūni-**	unit	VI.	**sext-**	sextet
	prīm-	primary	VII.	**sept-**	September
II.	**du-**	duet	VIII.	**oct-**	octopus
	bi-	bicycle		**octāv-**	octave
	second-	secondary	IX.	**novem-**	November
III.	**tri-**	triple	X.	**dec-**	decade
IV.	**quadr-**	quadruped		**decim-**	decimal
	quārt-	quarter			
V.	**quīnt-**	quintet			

Try these:

1. If a *sextet* is a group of six, how many members make up a *quartet?*

   _____.
   A group of five is a _____. A group of seven is a

   _____.
   A group of eight is an _____. A group of two is a

   _____.

2. Remember the *foot* root-forms **pod-** and **ped-?** Another root-form for *foot* is **pus-.**

   Now give the root meaning of *octopus:* _____ + _____.
   Poly- means "many." The Romans called an octopus a **polypus.** Why?

3. **Prīm-** can mean "highest" as well as "first." A *prima ballerina* in a dance company is not a beginner. She's the best dancer, the one who is first, the star. On the other hand, *primary school* is the first school you attend but not the highest. In fact, *secondary school* (high school) is higher than primary school. Since you attend it later, after *primary* school, it's called *secondary* school.

   Look up these words from **prīm-** in a dictionary and write their meanings here:

   primitive _____

   principal _____

Word Games

The Eights Have It

OCTAVE   OCTET   OCTOPUS
OCTAGON   OCTOBER   OCTOGENARIAN

1. Eight musicians playing together form an _____.

2. When the Roman calendar had ten months, the eighth was _____.

Mars/March

3. "Do, Re, Mi, Fa, Sol, La, Ti, Do" makes a musical _____.

4. An eight-sided figure is an _____.

5. A marine animal with eight tentacles is called an _____.

6. Claudia's grandfather is 80 years old; he's an _____.

Juno/June

Match It Up

1. septet   _____ a musical composition for three instruments

2. primate   _____ one of five babies born at the same time

3. decimate   _____ sounding as one, in agreement

4. trio   _____ a reciting of prayers for nine days in a row

5. unisonal   _____ a group of seven

6. duplicate _____ one-fourth of a gallon

7. quintuplet _____ to kill one in every ten

8. quart   _____ highest order of animal in biological classification

9. novena   _____ a copy or double

Julius
Caesar/July

Augustus
Caesar/August

Deī Rōmānī

Fābella: Ad Templum

Persōnae: Cornēlia, Lūcius, Claudia

Lucius and Claudia have had a great time showing their cousin Cornelia the sights of Rome. On her last morning in the city, Cornelia visits the *Temple of Jupiter Maximus* (The Greatest) on the Capitoline Hill. She admires the carved statues of Jupiter and other gods and goddesses at the top of the temple.

CORNĒLIA: *(looking at the large temple)* Templum est magnum! (1)
    (pointing to a statue) Statua est magna! Quis est? (2)

CLAUDIA: Iuppiter est. Iuppiter est rēx deōrum. Iuppiter est deus maximus. (3)

CORNĒLIA: *(pointing to another statue)* Dea est. Quis est? (4)

LŪCIUS: Iūnō est. Iūnō est rēgīna deōrum. Iūnō est dea maxima. (5)

The three cousins hurry back to the house so that Cornelia won't miss her carriage. Lucius and Claudia promise to visit Cornelia in the summer.

CORNĒLIA: Tibi grātiās agō, Lūcī! Tibi grātiās agō, Claudia! Rōma est maxima! (6)
    Rōma est optima! Rōmae habitāre volō. Valēte! (7)

LŪCIUS ET CLAUDIA: *(waving)* Valē, Cornēlia! Valē, amīca! (8)

Vocabulary Help:

(3) **rēx deōrum** king of the gods
    deus god
(4) **dea** goddess
(5) **rēgīna deōrum** queen of the gods
(7) **optima** the best
    Rōmae habitāre volō I want to live in Rome

Duodecim Deī et Deae

The Greeks and the Romans portrayed their gods and goddesses like human beings, but with superhuman powers and everlasting life. Here are the twelve most important. They were called the Olympians as a group because the Romans believed they lived on Mount Olympus in Greece. Find the picture that matches the description and place the *Latin name* of the god or goddess in the blank.

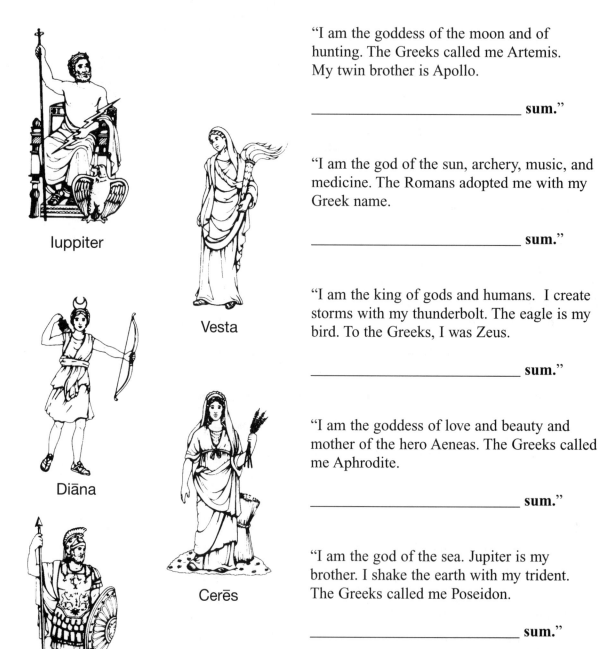

Iuppiter

Vesta

Diāna

Cerēs

Mars

"I am the goddess of the moon and of hunting. The Greeks called me Artemis. My twin brother is Apollo.

_____ sum."

"I am the god of the sun, archery, music, and medicine. The Romans adopted me with my Greek name.

_____ sum."

"I am the king of gods and humans. I create storms with my thunderbolt. The eagle is my bird. To the Greeks, I was Zeus.

_____ sum."

"I am the goddess of love and beauty and mother of the hero Aeneas. The Greeks called me Aphrodite.

_____ sum."

"I am the god of the sea. Jupiter is my brother. I shake the earth with my trident. The Greeks called me Poseidon.

_____ sum."

"I am the queen of gods and humans. Jupiter is my husband, and I'm proud as a peacock. The Greeks called me Hera.

_____ **sum.**"

"I am the god of war and father of Romulus and Remus. I wear armor to defend Rome. The Greeks called me Ares.

_____ **sum.**"

"I am the goddess of the sacred flame that burns forever in my temple, to keep Rome safe forever. The Greeks called me Hestia.

_____ **sum.**"

"I am the messenger god with winged sandals and helmet. I protect travelers. The Greeks called me Hermes.

_____ **sum.**"

"I am the goddess of the harvest and agriculture. The Greeks called me Demeter.

_____ **sum.**"

"I am the god of metalworking. I hammer out thunderbolts for Jupiter and weapons for heroes. The Greeks called me Hephaistos.

_____ **sum.**"

"I am the goddess of wisdom, war, and weaving. I sprang full-grown from the head of my father Jupiter. The Greeks called me Athena.

_____ **sum.**"

Apollō

Neptūnus

Mercurius

Volcānus

Venus

Minerva

Iūnō

Nōmen, Nōmen

The *English* spelling of the names of the Roman deities (gods and goddesses) is sometimes different from the Latin spelling:

Jupiter	**Juno**	**Apollo**	**Diana**	**Mercury**	**Vesta**
Vulcan	**Ceres**	**Neptune**	**Venus**	**Mars**	**Minerva**

Fill in the charts below with the English and Latin names.

Deae Rōmānae		Deī Rōmānī	
English	**Latin**	**English**	**Latin**
Juno	Iūnō	_____	_____
_____	_____	_____	_____
_____	_____	_____	_____
_____	_____	_____	_____
_____	_____	_____	_____

What is the Latin ending on the names of three gods that changes or

disappears in English? _____.

What is the Latin ending on the names of three goddesses that stays the same

in English? _____.

Word Play

Fill in the blanks with the following words:

VOLCANIC   MERCURIAL   MARTIAL   CEREAL   JOVIAL

1. If you're speedy like Mercury, you're _____.

2. If you're made of grain, which Ceres causes to grow, you're _____.

3. If you learn how to fight like the god Mars, you study _____ arts.

4. If you're heated up like Vulcan's furnace, you're _____ rock.

5. If you're merry like Jove (another name for Jupiter), you're _____.

Astronomy: The Planets

As each of the eight planets in our solar system (besides Earth) was discovered by scientists, it received the name of a Roman deity.

Fill in the four planets named after gods we have already studied:

1. _____ 2. _____ 3. _____ 4. _____

Fill in the planet named after a goddess. 5. _____

The three remaining planets are named after other gods:

Sāturnus, a very ancient Roman god identified with the Greek god Kronos, father of Jupiter. He had a huge temple at one end of the Forum, directly below the Temple of Jupiter on the Capitoline Hill. Part of the temple is still standing today.

6. _____

Plūtō, god of the underworld and brother of Neptune and Jupiter. He ruled over

dead souls below the earth. His Greek name was Hades. 7. _____

Ūranus, a Greek sky god who was adopted by the Romans. He was Jupiter's

grandfather. 8. _____

The planets revolve around the *sun*. They belong to the *solar* system. What's the connection? The English word *sun* is from the German **Sonne,** which means "sun." The English word *solar* is from the Latin **sōl,** which means "sun." Sometimes the Romans called the God of the Sun **Sōl** instead of **Apollō!**

Legāmus!

Planētae

Terra est planēta nostra.   (1)
Sāturnus et Venus quoque sunt planētae.   (2)
Sunt novem planētae.   (3)
Omnēs planētae circum sōlem sē revolvunt.   (4)
Lūna circum Terram sē revolvit.   (5)

Saturn

Vocabulary Help:

(1) **nostra** our
(2) **quoque** also
(3) **sunt** there are

(4) **omnēs** all
    circum around
    sē revolvunt revolve

(5) **lūna** moon

Respondē Latīnē: ～～～～～～～～～～～～～～～～～～～～～～

1. Quid est Terra?

2. Quot *(how many)* planētae sunt?

3. Quid circum Terram sē revolvit?

Review I

Vērum aut Falsum?

Here are twelve sentences in Latin. Find the **six** that are *true* and put an *X* next to each of those. Then translate the *true* sentences in the spaces provided. The first one is done for you.

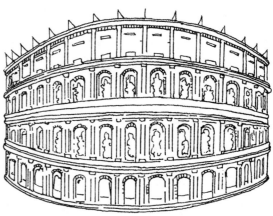

1. ____X____ Claudia est puella Rōmāna.

2. _____ Lūcius est puer Rōmānus.

3. _____ Lūcius est discipula.

4. _____ Cornēlia est puer.

5. _____ Rōmulus est prīmus Rōmānus.

6. _____ Iānuārius est secundus mēnsis.

7. _____ Ūnus plūs sex sunt septem.

8. _____ Duo multiplicātum per quīnque sunt octō.

9. _____ Quattuor dīvīsum per duo sunt trēs.

10. _____ Novem minus quattuor sunt quīnque.

11. _____ Italia est in Āfricā.

12. _____ Rōma est in Italiā.

_____ 1. Claudia is a Roman girl. _____

_____

_____

_____

_____

_____

Quis Sum?

Match the name of each famous character with the event:

1. I founded the city of Rome. **Quis sum?**"

   "_____ es."

2. "I burned my right hand to prove Romans are brave.

   Quis sum?" "_____ es."

3. "I was so powerful that my fellow citizens murdered me.

   Quis sum?" "_____ es."

4. "I held off a whole army by myself on a bridge.

   Quis sum?" "_____ es."

5. "I landed in Italy with the help of my mother Venus.

   Quis sum?" "_____ es."

6. "I was the first emperor of Rome. **Quis sum?**"

   "_____ es."

Augustus

Horātius

Aenēas

Rōmulus

Iūlius Caesar

Mūcius Scaevola

Quid Est?

Place the number of the famous sight in Rome next to its description:

1. Colosseum   _____ the center of business and government activity

2. Circus Maximus   _____ a place for cleansing, exercise, and relaxation

3. Forum Romanum   _____ a wealthy district of Rome

4. Bath of Trajan   _____ a large amphitheater for gladiatorial contests

5. Appian Way   _____ the largest course for chariot races

6. Theater of Marcellus _____ the road from southern Italy to Rome

7. Palatine Hill   _____ place where plays were performed

Deī et Deae

Pick the letter of the choice in Column B that best describes the god or goddess in Column A.

Column A

1. Iuppiter   _____
2. Iūnō   _____
3. Apollō   _____
4. Cerēs   _____
5. Minerva   _____
6. Mercurius   _____
7. Diāna   _____
8. Mars   _____
9. Venus   _____
10. Neptūnus   _____
11. Vesta   _____
12. Volcānus   _____

Column B

a. Queen of the gods

b. God of the sea

c. Goddess of agriculture

d. King of the gods

e. Goddess of wisdom and weaving

f. God of war

g. Goddess of love

h. God of metalworking and weapons

i. Goddess of the flame in the temple

j. God of the sun and music

k. Goddess of the moon and hunting

l. Messenger god

Cross It Out!

Cross out the one item in each list that does not belong with the others.

1. Romance languages: French, Spanish, German, Italian, Portuguese
2. Nations in the Roman Empire: Italia, Gallia, Aegyptus, China, Hispānia
3. English words from **ūni-:** unite, unique, under, unicorn, unicycle
4. Roman numerals: X, I, V, Q, C
5. People in the Forum: shoppers, senators, soldiers, acrobats, movie stars
6. City life in ancient Rome: crowds, fast food, street lights, noise, buildings
7. Latin words describing people: **magistra, camera, discipula, puella, fēmina**
8. Mythological monsters: Saturn, Harpy, Minotaur, Scylla, Cyclops

Number Exchange

Fill in the blanks:

1. If a duet is a group of *two,* a quartet is a group of _____, and a

   quintet is a group of _____. What is the word for a group of

   eight? It is an _____.

2. Although people are *bipeds,* many animals are *quadrupeds* because they

   have _____.

3. If a person speaks *two* languages, she is bilingual. If she speaks *three*

   languages, she is _____.

4. If a biennial event takes place every *two* years, a triennial event takes place

   every _____ years, and a quadrennial event every

   _____ years.

5. A quadrangle is a shape with *four* angles. What is the word for a shape

   with *three* angles? _____.

6. If triplets are *three* babies born at the same time, quintuplets are

   _____ babies born at the same time, and quadruplets are

   _____ babies born at the same time.

7. If October used to be the *eighth* month in the Roman calendar, November

   was the _____ month. What was the *tenth* month called?

   _____.

8. How many wheels does a bicycle have? _____ Add *cycle* to the

   Latin root-forms for *one* and *three* to make two more *cycle* words in

   English: one-wheeler _____, three-wheeler _____.

Arbor Verbōrum

Each branch of this Latin number tree contains English words from Latin roots. Find the *correct* English word to complete each sentence below. You will not use all the choices.

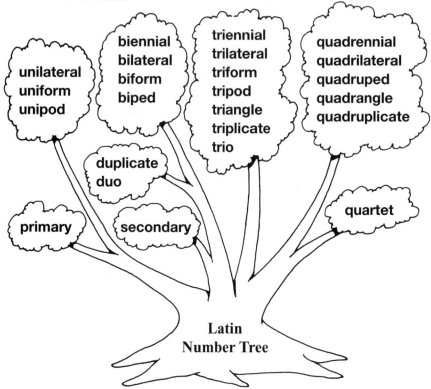

Latin Number Tree

1. The first school you attend is called _____ school.

2. Four people playing music together make up a _____.

3. If a trio is a group of three, a group of two is a _____.

4. Because it has only one foot, a clam is called a _____.

5. An event that takes place every three years is _____.

6. A figure with four angles is called a _____.

7. If cookies have one size and shape, they are _____.

8. If you make three copies of a letter, you copy it in _____.

9. A peace treaty signed by two sides is a _____ agreement.

10. A person who can change his shape into that of a wolf is _____.

Familia Claudī

In this unit, you will:

meet the family of Claudius, a Roman senator
meet Quintus, a freedman
look inside a Roman house and apartment building
discuss slavery and freedom in Rome
describe yourself and your family in Latin
sing a Latin song about the family
perform a Roman ceremony in Latin
read Latin stories and myths
learn many English words that come from Latin

© Scott Foresman - Addison Wesley

Familia Claudī I

Family Members

Here are the four members of Claudius' immediate family. Fill in the blanks. Choose your answers from the following list:

puer   **puella**   **vir**   **fēmina**   **soror**
pater   **māter**   **frāter**   **fīlius**   **fīlia**

Lūcius est _____.

Lūcius est _____.

Lūcius est _____.

Lūcius

Claudius est _____.

Claudius est _____.

Claudius

Antōnia est _____.

Antōnia est _____.

Antōnia

Claudia est _____.

Claudia est _____.

Claudia est _____.

Claudia

The Roman Family

The English word *family* comes from the Latin word **familia,** which means "household." The **paterfamiliās** (father of the household) was in charge of his own **familia,** and he had absolute power. In addition to the immediate family members, the **familia** would include slaves, other relatives, and anyone else who depended on the **paterfamiliās.** When a son became an adult or got married, he might leave his father's household and begin a new one. After a daughter married, she joined the **familia** of her new husband.

There were many types of households in ancient Rome, just as there are many types of American families. Here are three Roman households. As you read, compare the life-styles and responsibilities of the Roman family members with your own.

Familia Egnātī

Pater: "Egnātius sum. I work long hours in a bakery to support my family. My wife, two sons, two daughters, and I live in rooms behind my shop."

Māter: "Aurēlia sum. I help my husband in his bakery but spend most of my time taking care of my family's needs: their food and clothing."

Fīlius Prīmus: "Marcus sum. My father sends my brother and me to a teacher every morning to learn how to read and write. He teaches us how to bake bread in the afternoons."

Fīlius Secundus: "Gāius sum. I wear a tunic all day now. When I'm about 16, I'll receive the white toga that only grown men may wear."

Fīlia Prīma: "Egnātia sum. I am 14 years old. Father and mother will choose a husband for me soon. Father has been saving money for my dowry."

Fīlia Secunda: "Egnātia Secunda sum. I spend all day with my mother. She teaches me sewing, weaving, cooking, and all the things I must know to be a good wife."

Familia Pūblicī

Paterfamiliās: "Pūblicius sum. My household is very large, with my wife, children, their families, and many slaves. We live in a large house in the city and spend summers in a villa in the country."

Wife of Paterfamiliās: "Cassia sum. I spend my days managing the household. I direct the slaves as they clean, shop, and cook."

Pater: "Servius Pūblicius sum. I am a wealthy young man, married ten years. I live in my parents' house, where my father, the **paterfamiliās,** is the absolute authority over me and my own family."

Māter: Iūlia Pūblicia sum. When I married ten years ago, I took my husband's name and became part of his household. I help my mother-in-law with the slaves."

Fīlius: "Sextus sum. I want to be a public official, like my grandfather. I'll have to study public speaking and Roman law."

Fīlia: "Pūblicia sum. I stay with my mother and grandmother most of the day and watch them directing the slaves. I play games with my friends. I have many dolls."

Familia Marī

Paterfamiliās: "Marius sum. I am a banker in Rome. I take care of financial matters for my sons. When I die, each son will start his own household."

Māter: "Octāvia sum. The banker is my third husband. My parents selected my first husband, but the marriage didn't last. My second husband was a soldier and was killed in battle."

Fīlius Prīmus: "Brūtus sum. I'm married and have three children of my own. Father has put me in charge of the farmlands he owns outside the city."

Fīlius Secundus: "Spurius sum. I live with my mother and stepfather. My real father was a brave soldier who was killed in a great battle. The banker adopted me as his own son."

Fīlia: "Maria sum. My parents send me to a teacher each morning. Most of the other students are boys, but I think girls should know how to read and write too."

Avunculus (Brother of Māter): "Quīntus Octāvius sum. I live with my sister and her husband, the banker. I invested much money in shiploads of merchandise that were stolen by pirates."

Fīlia of Avunculus: "Octāvia sum. My father and I are living with my aunt until my father can earn enough to buy us a house. My aunt takes good care of me."

Questions to Think About

1. Who, according to Roman law, was responsible for a family? Is this true today?
2. How did the different family members (**pater, māter, fīlius, fīlia**) spend their time? How does this compare with family members today?
3. Did Roman children have to attend school? Who decided? Is this true today?

Word Play

1. Words belong to groups just as people belong to families. Fill in the answers to the following questions to make one word group:

   If *maternal* means "motherly, like a mother," what does *paternal* mean?

   Paternal means _____.

   How do you say "brotherly, like a brother"? _____.

   Think of the Latin word for *sister*. How do you say "sisterly"?

   (Hint: Leave out the *n* this time) _____.

   Here is another word group to make:

   If *maternity* means "motherhood," what does *paternity* mean?

   Paternity means _____.

   Fraternity means _____.

   Sorority means _____.

   You may know other meanings for *fraternity* and *sorority*. See if you can connect them with the basic meaning you put in the blanks.

2. To form word groups, we take the Latin root-form and add an ending to it. The endings we added above are **-al** and **-ity**. There are many other endings for the roots we have learned. For each word in the left column below, fill in a comparable word in the right column:

pater, patr-	m**āter, mātr-**
paterfamilias	materfamilias
patriarch	
patron	matron
patrimony	

   It is easy to see the spelling relationship between each word pair. But what do the words mean? As you discuss these words with your teacher, keep in mind a major difference between the father and the mother in the Roman family: The father held the power and money, while the mother cared for the children at home. Do the meanings of the modern English words in the chart illustrate this difference between male and female roles? Consider this: If a woman gives money to a museum, she becomes a *patron*, a person with the power of the **pater!**

Familia Claudī II

Slavery in Ancient Rome

In the United States, the word *slavery* brings to mind the difficult period before the Civil War, when people from Africa were bought and sold by slave-traders, mostly to work on farms, where they were often treated badly. In ancient times, for *millions* of people all over the Mediterranean world, slavery was very common. The Romans considered it a normal and acceptable part of life. There were many kinds of slaves, and they had an important role in the everyday activities of the city. Try to keep this idea in mind as you learn about slavery in ancient Rome.

How Many Slaves Were in a *Familia?*

Mopsus and Amabilis were part of the **familia** of Claudius. Since Claudius was a middle-class man, he would have at least 20 or 30 slaves in his city house. Even a very poor man often owned at least one slave. A wealthy man might keep a city house with 200 slaves and several farms with hundreds more. During the Roman Empire, the number of slaves in Rome was very large—about half of the total population.

How Did a Person Become a Slave?

Slaves were sent to the city of Rome from all parts of the Empire. They were usually ordinary people who were taken prisoner by the conquering Roman army or by pirates. There were slaves of both sexes and all ages. Some were highly educated or skilled in a trade. The enormous Roman Empire included peoples from many different countries and races. When prisoners came to Rome as slaves, they had to leave behind their families, their jobs, and the language and customs of their native country. They were forced to adjust to the Roman style of life.

What Rights Did Slaves Have?

Prisoners were sold in slave markets by slave-traders. Once they were bought, they became the property of their master. They had no legal rights. They could not marry, vote, or wear the toga of citizenship. Their children were born into slavery and belonged to the master. If a slave tried to escape, he might be branded on his forehead with the letters FUG, short for **fugitīvus,** which means "runaway."

Some masters were quite cruel to their slaves, while others were considerate and kind. Since slaves needed to be properly fed, dressed, and rested in order to work well, it would be foolish for a master to harm his slaves and make them unfit for their tasks. Slaves usually lived in the same house as the master and his family. Although they weren't free, sometimes these household slaves became very close to the family and over the years were treated with affection.

What Did Slaves Do?

Slaves did all kinds of work. Country slaves worked the land owned by their master. Their life was hard—they worked long hours in the fields. Slaves living in the city house worked in teams with specific duties—cleaning, cooking, child care, clothing. Others were personal family attendants, going everywhere with their masters or mistresses. Still others might work in factories, teach school, make handcrafted objects, take care of the city parks, or become actors and musicians. The very strongest were sometimes trained as gladiators.

As they worked, slaves mingled with free men. They went shopping, attended shows in the theater, and participated in religious festivals at the temples. They did not wear special clothes. A foreigner visiting Rome would not be able to tell the slaves apart from the poor free working men. Slaves blended into the business and life of the great city.

Time Traveler: A Slave in Rome

Imagine you are from a foreign country that has been conquered by the Romans. You have just been sent to Rome to be sold at auction as a slave. Describe your feelings, the life you left behind, the master who buys you, and what kind of life you can expect.

Word Play

1. You have seen that one Latin root gives us many English words. **Servus/serva, serv-** is a good example. Fill in the chart with as many words and their definitions as you can:

Latin Word and Root	English Word	Meaning of the English Word
servus/serva serv-	_____	_____
	_____	_____
	_____	_____
	_____	_____
	_____	_____
	_____	_____
	_____	_____

2. Add the following English word to the *-al* word group: *filial,* from **filius/filia, fili-,** "like a son or daughter." The name of the family dog, Rex, means "king." From the Latin word **rēx, rēg-** we get English *regal.* Notice the *-al* ending. What do you think *regal* means?

   It means "like a _____."

3. The ending *-ine* means the same thing as *-al,* "related to" or "like." It is used with Latin roots for animal names. For example, *canine* means "like a dog," from **canis, can-.** Think of Bella. What does *feline* mean? To make the English word, add *-ine* to each of these roots:

Latin	English	
canis, can- *dog*	canine	like a dog
leō, leōn- *lion*	_____	like a lion
asinus, asin- *donkey*	_____	like a donkey
porcus, porc- *pig*	_____	like a pig
aquila, aquil- *eagle*	_____	like an eagle

Familia Deōrum et Deārum

The twelve Olympian gods, and other gods important to the Romans, like Pluto and Saturn, were related to each other. The relationships were complicated. For example, Jupiter and Juno were brother and sister as well as husband and wife. The gods lived by different rules from the human beings they ruled over. Here is a diagram of some of the family ties. Names are given in Latin.

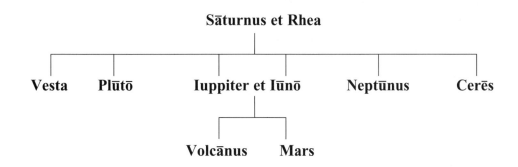

Sāturnus et Rhea

Vesta   **Plūtō**   **Iuppiter et Iūnō**   **Neptūnus**   **Cerēs**

Volcānus   **Mars**

Jupiter and the goddess Leto were the parents of the twins **Apollō** and **Diāna.** Jupiter also was the father of **Minerva,** born from his head, of **Venus,** born from the sea foam, and of **Mercurius,** whose mother was the goddess Maia.

Using the information above and your knowledge of the twelve Olympian deities, fill in the blanks to indicate the family relationships of the gods and goddesses:

1. Iuppiter et Neptūnus et _____Plūtō_____ sunt frātrēs.

2. Iūnō et Vesta et _____ sunt sorōrēs.

3. _____ est māter Volcānī.

4. Apollō et _____ sunt frāter et soror.

5. Volcānus et _____ sunt frātrēs.

6. Sāturnus est _____ Vestae et Neptūnī et Plūtōnis.

7. _____ est fīlia Sāturnī et Rheae. *(Choose one of three.)*

8. Iuppiter est _____ Sāturnī et Rheae.

9. Minerva est _____ Iovis *(of Jupiter).*

10. _____ et _____ sunt parentēs Iovis et Iūnōnis.

Word Game

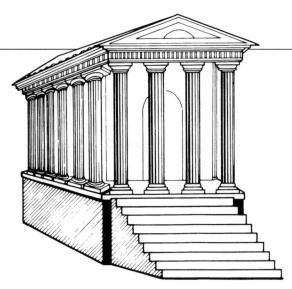

This is a Roman temple in the Doric style. Lucius and Claudia want to climb the stairs to the top. You can help them by marking the answers to the sentences either TRUE or FALSE.

1. _____ The male leader of a tribe is known as the *matriarch*.

2. _____ Mothers-to-be often buy clothes in *maternity* shops.

3. _____ Slaves always have *regal* living quarters.

4. _____ At colleges some young men join *sororities*.

5. _____ *Fraternal* feelings are the feelings Lucius had for Claudia.

6. _____ Lions, tigers, and cougars are *felines*.

7. _____ A *patron* of a store has the money to buy something in it.

8. _____ Your father's sister is your *maternal* relative.

9. _____ A person who is *servile* in manner is probably a king.

10. _____ *Canine* teeth are sharp and pointed like a dog's teeth.

11. _____ Before the Civil War, slaves were in a condition of *servitude*.

12. _____ To identify the *paternity* of a new litter of puppies, you have to discover which dog was the father.

Now that you have answered all the questions, you will find out if the children reached the top. For every answer that you marked TRUE, move UP *two* steps. For every answer you marked FALSE, move DOWN *one* step. There were nine steps. DID THEY MAKE IT?

Quīntus Lībertus

Language Discovery

Write the translation of each sentence below in the space provided. You have heard the first two in class.

Quīntus est lībertus. _____ Quintus (is) a freedman. _____

Mopsus est servus. _____

Quīntus est vir. _____

Mopsus est vir. _____

Antōnia est fēmina. _____

Amābilis est fēmina. _____

Circle the translation of **est** in each English sentence above.
Here are new sentences. Write the translation of each:

Quīntus et Mopsus sunt virī. _____

Antōnia et Amābilis sunt fēminae. _____

Circle the translation of **sunt** in each English sentence above.

Fill in each sentence below with either **est** or **sunt:**

1. Claudius _____ pater.

2. Claudius et Lūcius _____ pater et fīlius.

3. Claudius et Quīntus _____ virī.

4. Claudia _____ puella.

5. Claudia et Lūcius _____ soror et frāter.

6. Claudia et Lūcius _____ fīliī *(children)*.

7. Bella et Rēx _____ animālia.

8. Bella _____ fēlēs.

By now you have probably figured out that **est** *(is)* is used with one person or thing, and **sunt** *(are)* with more than one. Here's another way to say this: The word **est** is singular. The word **sunt** is plural.

Nouns—words that are labels for persons and things—are also singular and plural. As you know, for most nouns in English, simply add *s* to the singular. Fill in the chart:

Singular	Plural
boy	_____
girl	_____
cat	_____

Sometimes the spelling changes when *s* is added. Fill in the chart:

butterfly	_____
story	_____
wife	_____

The situation can get more complicated. Fill in the chart:

man	_____
woman	_____
child	_____
fish	_____ (CAREFUL!!)

Latin usually shows a difference in the endings between singular and plural nouns. Here are lists of nouns you know (look how many!), along with their plurals:

1		2		3	
Singular	**Plural**	**Singular**	**Plural**	**Singular**	**Plural**
puella	puellae	puer	puerī	pater	patrēs
fēmina	fēminae	vir	virī	māter	mātrēs
līberta	lībertae	lībertus	līberti	frāter	frātrēs
fīlia	fīliae	fīlius	fīliī	soror	sorōrēs
serva	servae	servus	servī	canis	canēs

What is the plural ending of the nouns in **Box 1?** Write it here _____.
Now pronounce the words in the box.

What is the plural ending of the nouns in **Box 2?** Write it here _____.
Now pronounce the words in the box.

Many Latin nouns form their plurals as in **Box 3.** Some of these nouns are masculine, like **pater,** and some are feminine, like **māter.**

Write the plural ending here _____. Now pronounce the words.

Circle the word that correctly completes each sentence below:

1. Claudia est (puella, puellae).
2. Mopsus est (servus, servī).
3. Claudius et Antōnia sunt (parēns, parentēs).
4. Claudius est (parēns, parentēs).
5. Antōnia et Amābilis sunt (fēmina, fēminae).
6. Rēx est (canis, canēs).
7. Claudius et Quīntus sunt (vir, virī).
8. Mopsus et Amābilis sunt (servus, serva, servī).
9. Lūcius est (discipulus, discipulī).

10. Lūcius et _____ sunt (discipulus, discipulī).

   (your Latin name)

Freedom at Last!

Imagine yourself as a Roman slave dreaming of freedom. There were several
different reasons you might be set free. It was common for a **paterfamiliās** to
free his older, loyal slaves when he died by making a statement in his will. A
slave might buy his freedom by saving up his money—either the money he
earned if he was allowed to work at a trade, or the allowance he would be
given for good service to his master. If a slave performed a deed of heroism, or
just worked hard and was loyal over the years, his master would free him out
of respect. But a master could not legally grant freedom until the slave was 30
years old.

   Once freed, a slave became a **lībertus,** a freedman (or **līberta,** freedwoman),
and took part of the former master's name. If the master was a Roman citizen,
the freed person, too, became a citizen. Although he and his children could not
run for high public office, like citizens who were born free, his grandchildren
would have the right to do so. The freedman was free to carry on his own
business and continued to depend on his former master as his patron. Some
freedmen were highly educated; others were fine craftsmen in the trade they
learned while they were slaves. Some became very wealthy and famous. Rich
or poor, freedmen mixed freely with both slaves and free-born citizens.

Fābella: Manūmissiō Quīntī

Persōnae: Quīntus, Claudius, Assertor *(Defender)*, Praetor *(Judge)*,
　　Amīcī Claudī *(Friends of Claudius)*, Antōnia

PRAETOR: Praetor sum. Quis est? *(points to Quintus)*　　　　　　　　　　(1)

ASSERTOR: Quīntus est. Quīntus nōn est servus Claudī.　　　　　　　　(2)

PRAETOR: *(turning to Claudius)* Vērum est? Quīntus nōn est servus tuus?　(3)

CLAUDIUS: Vērum est.　　　　　　　　　　　　　　　　　　　　(4)

PRAETOR: *(to Quintus)* Venī, Quīnte. *(Quintus approaches the praetor and kneels.*　(5)
　　The praetor taps him on the head with a rod.) Es līber, Quīnte.　　(6)

CLAUDIUS: *(to Quintus)* Gere pilleum, Quīnte. *(He puts the cap of freedom on*　(7)
　　Quintus' head. Quintus stands up.)

AMĪCĪ CLAUDĪ: Quīntus est lībertus! Quīntus est lībertus!　　　　　(8)

QUĪNTUS: Sum lībertus. Tibi grātiās agō, domine *(shakes Claudius' hand).*　(9)
　　Grātiās agō, domina *(shakes Antonia's hand).*　　　　　　　　(10)

ANTŌNIA: Bonus es, Quīnte. Venīte, omnēs. Cēna magna domī est.　(11)

Vocabulary Help:

(2) **nōn** not
servus Claudī the slave of
　Claudius
(3) **Vērum est?** Is it true?
tuus your
(6) **līber** free
(7) **gere pilleum** wear the **pilleus**

(9) **tibi grātiās agō** I thank you
domine master
(10) **domina** mistress
(11) **bonus** a good man
omnēs everybody
cēna magna a big dinner
domī at home

Word Search: Familia Claudī

Find and circle the **Latin** words for the English words listed to the right. Words
may go across, down, or on the diagonal, but they are never backward.

```
S F P U E R S
E I M A S P O
R L A R T U R
V I T E B E O
U I E X I L R
S E R V A L I
F E L E S A E
```

1. boy
2. girl
3. female slave
4. male slave
5. sister
6. father
7. mother
8. cat
9. "King"
10. children (son and daughter)

Mini-Review II

Quis Sum?

Identify the speaker in each of the following as **P—pater, M—māter, FS—fīlius, FA—fīlia, S—servus** or **serva,** or **L—lībertus.**

1. _____ Pirates captured me. Now I'm being sold at an auction.

2. _____ I am learning the skills for being a good wife from my mother.

3. _____ After I go to school in the morning, I work in my father's bakery.

4. _____ I have the power of life and death over each family member by law.

5. _____ I put on the **pilleus** at the end of my manumission ceremony.

6. _____ My husband is rich. I manage the household and direct the slaves.

7. _____ I work hard in the fields. My master is very harsh.

8. _____ I will be allowed to wear the toga of manhood soon.

9. _____ Father is saving for my dowry and will choose my husband soon.

10. _____ I'm a Roman senator. I own three houses in the city.

Singular or Plural I

First fill in each sentence below with either **est** or **sunt.**
Then translate the sentence into English.

1. Antōnia _____ māter. _____

2. Mopsus et Amābilis _____ servī. _____

   _____

3. Rēx _____ canis. _____

4. Claudia et Lūcius _____ soror et frāter. _____

   _____

Singular or Plural II

Circle the form of the noun that completes
each sentence correctly.

1. Lūcius est (puer/puerī).

2. Līvia et Claudia sunt (amīca/amīcae).

3. Quīntus et Mopsus sunt (vir/virī).

4. Amābilis est (serva/servae).

5. Claudius et Antōnia sunt (parēns/parentēs).

6. (Antōnia/Antōnia et Amābilis) sunt fēminae.

Word Power

Here are eight English words based on Latin words you have learned.
Circle the Latin root-form in each.

CANINE	REGAL	MATRIMONY	PATERFAMILIAS
LIBERTY	FILIAL	SERVANT	FRATERNAL

Complete the following sentences using these words.

1. The millionaire lived like a king; he lived in _____ splendor.

2. The minister at the wedding said, "I join you in holy

   _____."

3. German shepherds are members of the _____ family.

4. The father who is the head of the household is the

   _____.

5. Lucius and Claudia treated their parents with _____
   devotion.

6. At the manumission ceremony, Claudius gave Quintus his

   _____.

7. The tired old man hired a _____ to clean his house.

8. Lucius and his best friend Publius were like brothers; they had

   _____ feelings for each other.

Domus Claudī

In Domō

This is a cut-away picture of Claudius' house.

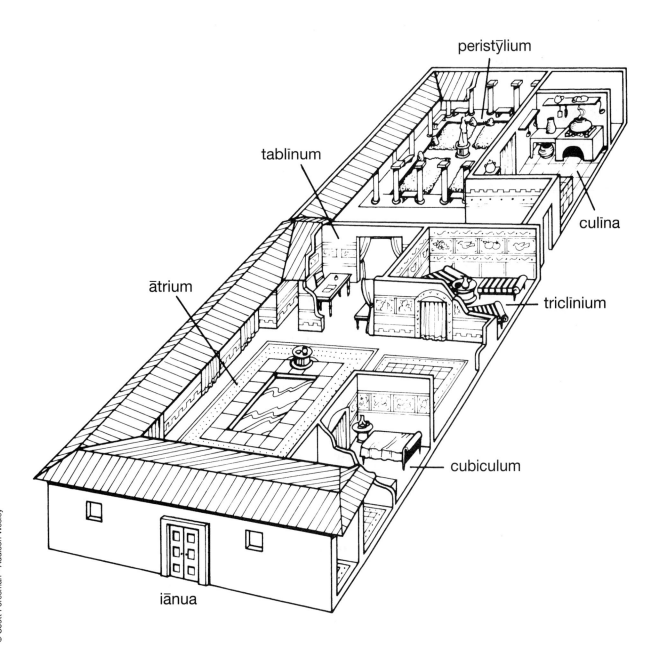

peristȳlium

tablīnum

culīna

ātrium

triclīnium

cubiculum

iānua

Quid Sum?

Fill in each blank below with the name of a room you see in the **domus** on page 57:

I am the main room of the house and the first room you enter. I have a small, shallow pool in my center to collect rainwater, which falls down from an opening in my ceiling directly above it. Although I have very little furniture, I am beautiful, with mosaic tiles on my floor and pictures of flowers, gods, and goddesses painted right on my walls. I have a few small windows high up, but sunlight shines in me from the roof opening. In one corner, I contain a small shrine with statues of the Claudian family gods for the **familia** to worship. Doorways covered with curtains lead from me to many rooms: at the front, to the shops my master rents out; at the sides, to the bedrooms; and in the back, to the family room, the dining room, and the hallway leading to the rest of the house.

Quid sum? _____

I am a very small room, but quite important. I contain a high wooden bed with a mattress stuffed with wool, an oil lamp, and a small dressing table. There is one small window high up in the wall. During the waking hours of the **familia,** I am never used, unless someone is sick.

Quid sum? _____

I am a popular room at dinner time. My walls are decorated with paintings of fruit and birds. I have a table in the middle, with *three* couches around it for people to lie on *(recline)* while they eat.

Quid sum? _____

I am the family living room where only the **familia** and special friends are welcome. My master sits at a table and studies his account books or writes letters in me. My front entrance faces the **ātrium,** while my back opens on the garden at the back of the house.

Quid sum? _____

I am the large, airy courtyard at the back of the house. I am completely open, with a big garden **(hortus)** at my center filled with statues, flowers, and fresh herbs and spices. I am surrounded by fluted columns that hold up the roof for the rooms around my sides: the kitchen, the slaves' bedrooms, the bathroom, and storage rooms. Rex likes to sleep in me, especially on hot nights. In the summer, the family dines in me and relaxes with friends.

Quid sum? _____

I have a stove built against one wall and a large brick oven. Water enters my sink from underground pipes that connect up with the city water supply. My master pays for this hookup. Mopsus cooks in me.

Quid sum? _____

Word Play

I. From the verb **habitat** come several English derivatives you may know. All have meanings connected to the meaning of the Latin stem, **habit-:** "live in," "dwell." Three are nouns (labels for things), one is a verb (action word), and four are adjectives (describing words). Here is a list:

Nouns	**Verbs**	**Adjectives**	
inhabitant	inhabit	inhabited	inhabitable
habitat		uninhabited	uninhabitable
habitation			

Fill in the blanks in the following four sentences with words from the **adjective** list, *without* looking up the meanings of the words in the dictionary. Look for hints in the sentences:

1. The new house is *able* to be lived *in.* It is _____.

2. The old house is *unable* to be lived *in.* It is _____.

3. The city house has a family living *in* it. It is _____.

4. The house in the ghost town is empty. It is _____.

Write the meaning of the prefix **un-** _____.

Now match the **nouns** and the **verb** in the list at the top with their meanings:

1. A person who lives in a place is an _____.

2. The natural environment or living place of an animal is its _____.

3. Claudia's house is her place of _____.

4. To live in a place is to _____ it.

II. Did you know? A **dominus** is someone belonging to the **domus,** from **dom-,** meaning "house" + **-īnus,** meaning "related to." He's the master of the **domus,** or simply, the boss, the master. The name of the **dominus** of

Mopsus and Amabilis is _____. A **domina** is the *mistress* of the

domus. The name of the slaves' **domina** is _____. Translate silently: **Dominus et domina habitant in domō.** When you *dominate* a person, you

act like a _____.

Fill in the chart with other English words from **domus.**

	English Word	**Meaning of the English Word**
domus *(house)*		
dom-	_____	_____
	_____	_____
domin-	_____	_____
	_____	_____

Fābella: Baucis et Philēmōn

The Romans valued hospitality, welcoming needy travelers into their homes. In this famous story, as told by the poet Ovid, a poor old married couple are the only ones in town to welcome two tired and hungry strangers seeking protection from a storm. The travelers turn out to be Jupiter and Mercury, disguised as ordinary people. For their kindness and generosity, Baucis and Philemon are rewarded by the gods.

Persōnae: Baucis, Philēmōn, Iuppiter, Mercurius

BAUCIS *(hearing a knock):* Audī, Philēmōn! Sunt virī ad iānuam.	(1)
PHILĒMŌN: Aperī iānuam, Baucis!	(2)
BAUCIS et PHILĒMŌN: Intrāte, virī bonī, casam nostram.	(3)
IUPPITER: Grātiās vōbīs agō. Dēfessus sum et ēsuriō.	(4)

Philemon prepares a simple stew from the little food she has and pours some drops of wine for the strangers.

BAUCIS: Spectā mīrāculum, Philēmōn. Vīnum in pōculīs crescit.	(5)
Cibus in mēnsā crescit. Hī virī sunt deī.	(6)
BAUCIS et PHILĒMŌN *(falling on their knees):* Magnī deī, grātiās	(7)
vōbīs agimus. Sedētis ad mēnsam nostram. Laetī sumus.	(8)
MERCURIUS: Bonī et amīcī nōbīs estis. Quid cupitis?	(9)
PHILĒMŌN: Cupiō cum Baucide semper esse.	(10)
BAUCIS: Cupiō cum Philēmone semper esse.	(11)
IUPPITER et MERCURIUS: Estō!	(12)

Instantly the tiny hut is changed into a magnificent marble temple covered in gold. The loving couple become the guardians of the temple and live well for many years. At the end, the gods turn them into trees with intertwining branches. Baucis and Philemon are together forever.

Vocabulary Help:

(1) **Audī** Listen!

(2) **Aperī** Open!

(3) **Intrāte** Enter!
casam hut

(4) **dēfessus** tired
ēsuriō I am hungry

(5) **Spectā** Look at. . .!
vīnum wine
pōculīs cups
crescit is increasing

(6) **cibus** food
hī these

(8) **sedētis** you are sitting
laetī happy

(9) **amīcī nōbīs** friendly to us
Quid cupitis? What do you desire?

(10) **cupiō** I desire, want
cum with
semper always
esse to be

(12) **Estō!** All right!

Language Discovery

1. Here are some of the nouns you have learned about the house:

1	2	3
culīn**a**	hort**us**	ātri**um**
iānua	mūrus	peristȳlium
fenestra		tablīnum
mēnsa		cubiculum
sella		triclīnium

Write two words for family members that have the same ending as the

nouns in the first list: _____ _____.

Write the ending _____. Circle it in the list.

Write two words for family members that have the same ending as the

nouns in the second list: _____ _____.

Write the ending _____. Circle it in the list.

The third list is new. The common ending is _____. Circle it.

Like **serva, fīlia,** and **puella,** the nouns in List 1 are feminine.
Like **servus, fīlius,** and **puer,** the nouns in List 2 are masculine.

You might ask, "How can a *door* be feminine?"
In Latin, and in *all* the Romance languages that come from it, every noun
is assigned a category, called **gender:**
   Nouns ending in *-us* are usually *masculine (m).*
   Nouns ending in *-a* are usually *feminine (f).*
   Nouns ending in *-um* are *neuter* (Latin for *neither*—neither
      masculine nor feminine!) *(n)*

Here are some new nouns. Label them *m, f,* or *n.*

lectus (bed) _____   **larārium** (family shrine) _____

lātrīna (bathroom) _____   **vīlla** (country house) _____

tēctum (roof) _____   **impluvium** (pool for rainwater) _____

2. You now know the Latin words (nouns) for things around the house and
   the people who live in the house, and you also know how to group them.
   The next step is to find a way to describe these people and these items.

   A word that describes a noun is called an **adjective.** Some English
   adjectives are: *pretty, ugly, kind, cowardly, big, little, angry, happy.*

   Write three more: _____.

   Write a sentence in English describing each room in the Roman house.
   Use two adjectives in your sentence. Underline each. For example:
      The atrium is <u>large</u> and <u>beautiful</u>.

      or, The atrium has <u>beautiful</u> pictures and <u>small</u> windows.

Īnsula Quīntī

Language Discovery

Compare these sentences in English and Latin:

The garden is <u>large</u>.   Hortus est <u>magnus</u>.
The kitchen is <u>large</u>.   Culīna est <u>magna</u>.
The atrium is <u>large</u>.   Ātrium est <u>magnum</u>.

The adjectives are underlined in the three sentences.

What happens to the adjective in English?_____ *It stays the same.* _____

What happens to the adjective in Latin?_____

Magnus, magna, and **magnum** are different forms of the same adjective with the base **magn-,** meaning "large." Only the ending changes.

Why does the ending change?
In Latin, adjectives and the nouns they describe are *partners*.
If the noun is *masculine* like **hortus,** so is the adjective—**magnus.**
If the noun is *feminine* like **culīna,** so is the adjective—**magna.**
If the noun is *neuter* like **ātrium,** so is the adjective—**magnum.**

Complete these sentences by circling the correct form of the Latin adjective, and then translate the sentence into English:

Villa est (magnus, (magna) magnum).

_____ *The country house is large* _____.

Mūrus est (magnus, magna, magnum).

_____.

Peristȳlium est (magnus, magna, magnum).

_____.

Scrībe Latīnē!

Here are some Latin adjectives:

magn**us,** magn**a,** magn**um**—large
parvus, parva, parvum—small
longus, longa, longum—long, tall
lātus, lāta, lātum—wide
altus, alta, altum—grown-up; high, deep
rīdiculus, rīdicula, rīdiculum—funny
pulcher, pulchra, pulchrum—beautiful
īrātus, īrāta, īrātum—angry

astūtus, astūta, astūtum—clever
stultus, stulta, stultum—stupid
bonus, bona, bonum—good
malus, mala, malum—bad
amīcus, amīca, amīcum—friendly
laetus, laeta, laetum—happy
trīst**is** *(m),* trīst**is** *(f),* trīst**e** *(n)*—sad
dēformis, dēformis, dēforme—ugly

Choose any *four* nouns you know (names of rooms, people, or classroom objects). Pick an adjective from the list above to describe each noun and use the two in a Latin sentence. You can do it!

Here are some examples:

Peristȳlium est lāt**um.**   Amābilis est pulchr**a.** (Remember, she is feminine.)
Servus est bon**us.**   Pater est alt**us.** (Remember, **pater** is masculine.)

1. _____

2. _____

3. _____

4. _____

Word Play

1. The English noun ending **-itude** is used with some of the adjectives you have learned. For example, **altus** *(high)* from the root **alt-** + **-itude** = *altitude:* When you fly in a plane, the pilot announces its *altitude* or height.

   Here are more **-itude** words. Figure out the meaning of each from the Latin adjective: *magnitude, longitude, latitude, pulchritude.*

2. The English verb ending **-ify** means "to make." For example, *magnify* means "to make large." What do these verbs mean?

   beautify _____   *verify* (**vēr-** "true") _____

3. Some English adjectives come directly from Latin. Figure out the meaning of these words: *irate, astute, ridiculous, deformed.*

4. Find the Latin adjectives in the list at the top of the page that give the following words in English: *magnificent, amicable, prolong, malicious, bonanza.*

Īnsula Rōmāna

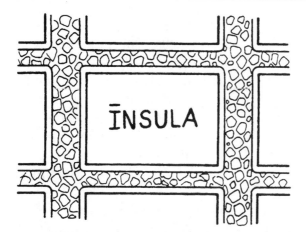

The word **īnsula** in Latin means "island." Roman cities were usually laid out in a grid pattern similar to modern cities. The section of buildings surrounded by four *streets* was called an **īnsula** (apartment block) just as an island is surrounded by *water*.

Most Romans were poor free-born citizens or freedmen. They did not own houses, but paid rent to live in apartment buildings. These buildings were often six or seven stories high. The first floor, street level, contained shops **(tabernae)** and perhaps a large apartment that cost more to rent. On the higher floors, the apartments became darker and smaller. The upper floors were frequently built of wood. Since there were no fire escapes, these cheaper apartments were dangerous firetraps.

Families crowded together, often in only one room, which had to serve for all purposes—eating, sleeping, and living. The rooms were hot, usually with only a single window for air. Beyond the first floor, there was no running water, bathroom facilities, or kitchen. An apartment dweller like Quintus would get his water from the public fountains, which were everywhere, and he would use public toilets, for which he paid a fee. After work, he would go to a public bath for cleansing and relaxation.

From the word **īnsula** come English *insulate*—to seal off, *insulated*—sealed off, and *insulation*—material used to seal something off. Fill in the blanks with one of these words:

The carpenter was hired to _____ the house.

He used _____ inside the walls to protect the house from the cold.

The house is now cosy and warm because it is _____.

Think about it: When we wrap ourselves in a blanket, we are like an island, completely surrounded. We are *insulated* or protected from the outside.

Did you know? Italy is a *peninsula,* from Latin **paene** *(almost)* and **īnsula.** Italy is an "almost island." Look at the map on p. 10 to see why!

Legāmus!

Flammae!

Claudius et Antōnia habitant in domō.	(1)
Amābilis et Mopsus habitant in domō.	(2)
Quīntus in domō nōn habitat. In īnsulā habitat. Quīntus est lībertus.	(3)
Post merīdiem Quīntus ambulat in viā ad īnsulam.	(4)
Laetus est quod sōl lūcet. Lībertus cantat et ambulat.	(5)
Subitō Quīntus fūmum videt. Flammās videt.	(6)
Flammae sunt magnae et altae.	(7)
"Flammae! Flammae!" clāmat Quīntus.	(8)
Vigilēs aquam portant. Flammās exstinguunt.	(9)
Quīntus est fortūnātus. Īnsula tūta est.	(10)

Vocabulary Help:

(4) **post merīdiem** in the afternoon
  ambulat is walking
  viā street
  ad īnsulam near his apartment
   block
(5) **quod** because
  sōl lūcet the sun is shining
(6) **subitō** suddenly
  fūmum smoke
  videt sees
  flammās flames

(8) **clāmat** shouts
(9) **vigilēs** firemen
  aquam water
  portant carry
  exstinguunt they extinguish
(10) **fortūnātus** lucky, fortunate
  tūta safe

Respondē Latīnē:

1. Ubi ambulat Quīntus?
2. Cūr *(why)* est Quīntus laetus?
3. Quid videt Quīntus? Quid clāmat?
4. Quī portant aquam?
5. Cūr est Quīntus fortūnātus?

Word Game

Javelin Contest

Help Romulus win the javelin contest. Complete each of the sentences below with a word from the list above.

1. A dog can be trained to live in a house; dogs are _____ animals.

2. It would be dangerous if an airplane pilot got dizzy at a high

   _____.

3. You can locate your city on a map if you know its longitude and

   _____.

4. When the slave was set free, he enjoyed his _____.

5. Beautiful Miss Piggy thinks she is an example of feminine

   _____.

6. The Romans did not have electricity, but their houses were

   _____.

7. The bad witch designed a _____ plan to kill Hansel and Gretel.

8. A goose-feather filled coat is very good _____ against the cold.

9. Trimalchio owned a very large and fancy house; it was

   _____.

10. Lucius laughed at Claudia; she looked _____ in her Juno costume.

Score 2 points for each correct answer. Romulus needed at least 14 points to win. DID HE SUCCEED?

Review II

Quis est ... ?

Mark an *X* next to the nouns that describe the character.

Example:

Lūcius est. . .   __X__ 1. puer   __X__ 2. fīlius   _____ 3. pater

_____ 4. soror   __X__ 5. frāter   __X__ 6. discipulus

I. Claudia est. . .   _____ 1. soror   _____ 2. puella   _____ 3. fīlia

_____ 4. puer   _____ 5. māter   _____ 6. frāter

II. Claudius est. . .   _____ 1. frāter   _____ 2. dominus   _____ 3. parēns

_____ 4. pater   _____ 5. servus   _____ 6. vir

III. Rēx est. . .   _____ 1. fēlēs   _____ 2. puella   _____ 3. animal

_____ 4. canis   _____ 5. dominus   _____ 6. amīcus

IV. Antōnia et Claudius sunt. . .

_____ 1. parēns   _____ 2. parentēs   _____ 3. virī

_____ 4. vir et fēmina   _____ 5. dominī   _____ 6. pater et māter

V. Quīntus et Mopsus sunt. . .

_____ 1. servī   _____ 2. lībertus et servus   _____ 3. virī

_____ 4. puerī   _____ 5. frāter et soror   _____ 6. dominī

Ubi Sum?

Match the description and the place in the Roman house.

1. _____ culīna   a. small room for sleeping

2. _____ ātrium   b. room with three couches and a table

3. _____ cubiculum   c. open courtyard in back of house

4. _____ triclīnium   d. private family room and study

5. _____ peristȳlium   e. bathroom

6. _____ hortus   f. pool for rainwater

7. _____ lātrīna   g. kitchen

8. _____ tablīnum   h. garden

9. _____ impluvium   i. main room in the front of the house

Legāmus!

Ad Mare

Pūblius est frāter Līviae et amīcus Lūcī.	(1)
Lūcius et Pūblius ambulant ad mare.	(2)
Claudia et Līvia quoque ambulant ad mare.	(3)
Quattuor līberī in aquā natant. Aqua est salsa et frīgida.	(4)
Pūblius laetus nōn est. Puer timidus ex aquā exit.	(5)
Lūcius laetus in aquā natat et lūdit.	(6)
Puellae laetae in aquā natant et lūdunt.	(7)
Subitō polypus pedem Lūcī capit. Puer clāmat, "Fer auxilium!"	(8)
Duae puellae puerum līberant.	(9)
"Multās grātiās!" Lūcius inquit. "Estis puellae bonae et fortēs."	(10)

Vocabulary Help:

(1) **frāter Līviae** Livia's brother
amīcus Lūcī a friend of Lucius
(2) **ad mare** near the sea
(4) **līberī** children
in aquā in the water
natant are swimming
salsa salty
frīgida cold
(5) **timidus** frightened
ex aquā exit leaves the water

(6) **lūdit** is playing
(8) **polypus** octopus
pedem Lūcī capit grabs the foot of Lucius
clāmat shouts
Fer auxilium! Help!
(9) **puerum līberant** free the boy
(10) **Multās grātiās** Many thanks!
inquit says
fortēs brave

Respondē Latīnē

1. Quis est Publius?
2. Ubi ambulant līberī?
3. Cūr *(Why)* nōn est Pūblius laetus?
4. Quid capit polypus?
5. Quae puerum līberant?

Seek and Find!

1. Find eleven adjectives in the story and ⟨circle⟩ them. Include the number words. Include **multās** *(many)*. Include all repeats. Hint: Look in lines 4, 5, 6, 7, 9, and 10.

2. Find nine *singular* verbs in the story and <u>underline</u> them. Include all repeats. Hints: Look in lines 1, 4, 5, 6, 8, and 10. Remember the *-t* ending.

3. Find five *plural* nouns in the story and put parentheses ( ) around them. Include **grātiās** *(thanks)*. Include all repeats. Hint: Look in lines 4, 7, 9, and 10.

Partners

⟨Circle⟩ the form of the adjective that makes a partnership with the noun. Remember to check the gender *(m, f, n)* and number (singular, plural) of the noun. Then translate the sentences.

1. Mopsus est (bonus, bona, bonum).
2. Ātrium est (pulcher, pulchra, pulchrum).
3. Amābilis est (laetus, laeta, laetum).
4. Fenestrae sunt (longa, longus, longae).
5. Puer est (malus, mala, malum).

1. _____

2. _____

3. _____

4. _____

5. _____

Crossword Puzzle

Clues: PERISTȲLIŌ   PATER
        RĒX   FAMILIA
        ĀTRIUM   DOMŌ
        MĀTER   ĪNSULĀ

1. Lucius et Claudia habitant in _____.

2. Antōnia est _____.

3. _____ Claudī habitat in domō.

4. _____ est magnum.

5. Hortus est in _____.

6. Quīntus habitat in _____.

7. Claudius est _____.

8. _____ est canis.

Roman Life-Styles

Put an *X* next to each statement that is TRUE.

1. _____ A slave's treatment depended primarily on the master.

2. _____ **Familia** is the Latin word for household or family.

3. _____ Roman children were required by law to attend school.

4. _____ Roman women had the same legal rights as American women.

5. _____ A slave might be able to buy his or her own freedom.

6. _____ Rich Roman households might have as many as 200 city slaves.

7. _____ Romans always sat up straight while they dined.

8. _____ A Roman house was organized around the **ātrium** and the **peristȳlium.**

9. _____ A freedman could hold high political office.

10. _____ Romans expected hosts and guests to treat each other with respect.

Word Game

dominate

inhabit

insulate

magnify

domesticate

liberate

ridicule

prolong

Chariot Race

Help the Roman Pacers win the chariot race. Complete each of the sentences below with a word from the list. Use the clues in parentheses ( ).

1. Claudius decided to (set free) _____ his slave Quintus.

2. Flavia's older brother Tiberius always tried to (control)

   _____ her.

3. The members of the household (live in) _____ a house.

4. We put on heavy coats to (protect) _____ ourselves against the cold.

5. A microscope is used to (make larger) _____ an object.

6. Felix tried to (housebreak) _____ his dog.

7. Lucius wanted to (laugh at) _____ Publius when he ran out of the cold water.

8. Do you want to (make longer) _____ the school year?

Check your answers with your teacher. Put a circle around every word in the list that you used correctly. Did you circle all the words and help the Pacers reach the goal?

Familia Deōrum et Deārum

I. Select the name that correctly completes each statement. Use each name only once. Then translate the sentence into English.

Cerēs   Iūnō   Apollō   Minerva   Iuppiter

1. Neptūnus et _____ sunt frātrēs.

   _____

2. Iuppiter et _____ sunt parentēs Volcānī.

   _____

3. Diāna et _____ sunt soror et frāter.

   _____

4. _____ est fīlia Iovis.

   _____

5. Vesta et _____ sunt sorōrēs.

   _____

II. Select the verb in parentheses that correctly completes each statement.

1. Iuppiter in Monte Olympō _____. (habitat, habitant)

2. Iūnō et Venus in Monte Olympō _____. (habitat, habitant)

3. Deī et deae in Monte Olympō _____ laetī. (est, sunt)

4. Minerva in Monte Olympō _____ laeta. (est, sunt)